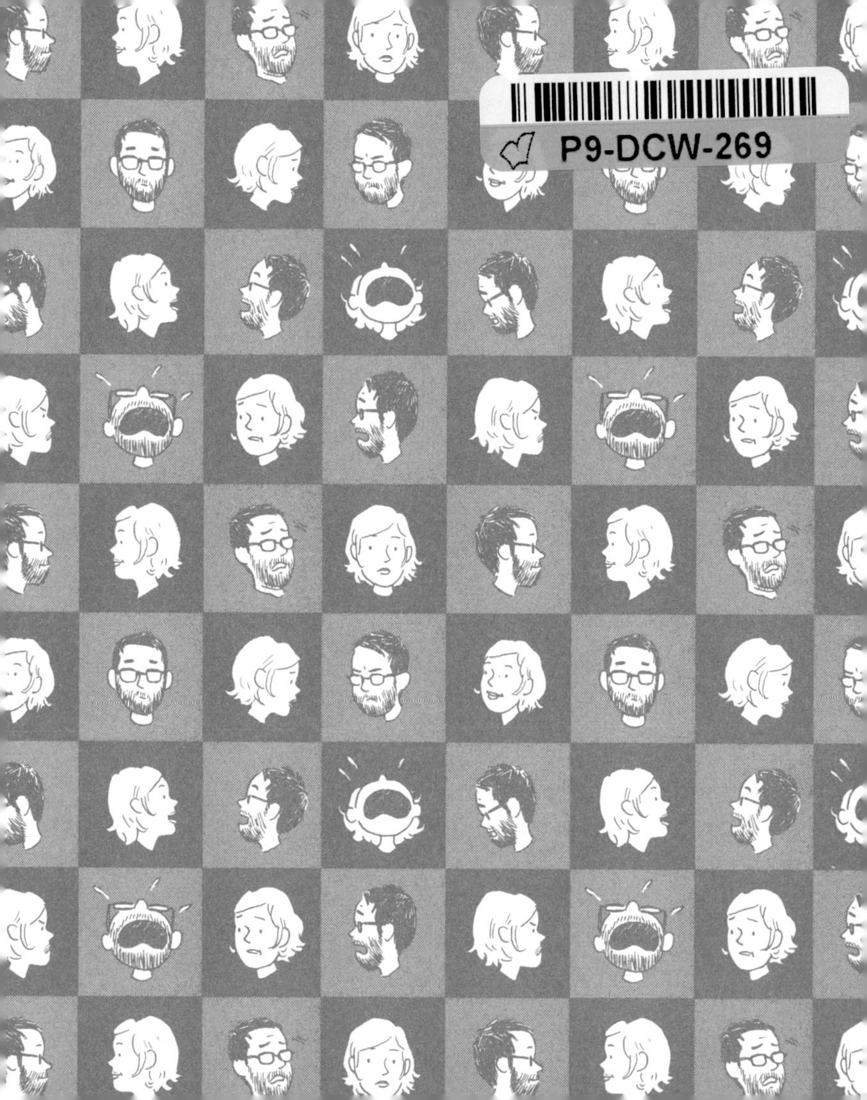

Scenes from an Impending Marriage

Prologue

SO... HOW DOES IT FEEL TO BE ENGAGED?

WEIRD.

YEAH.

AFTER ALL THIS LONG-DISTANCE DATING AND EVERYTHING, IT FEELS... PEACEFUL. IT'S NICE.

YEAH.

OKAY! SO THE FIRST THING WE NEED TO DO IS PICK A DAY, RIGHT? SPRING IS TOO SOON, SUMMER'S TOO HOT FOR YOU, SO MAYBE EARLY FALL WOULD BE BEST.

ACTUALLY, WE SHOULD PROBABLY LOOK AT VENUES FIRST. OR MAYBE WE SHOULD START WITH THE GUEST LIST.

THAT WAY WE'LL KNOW HOW MUCH--

UH, SORRY... QUICK QUESTION:

ANY CHANCE YOU'D WANT TO ELOPE?

Scenes from an

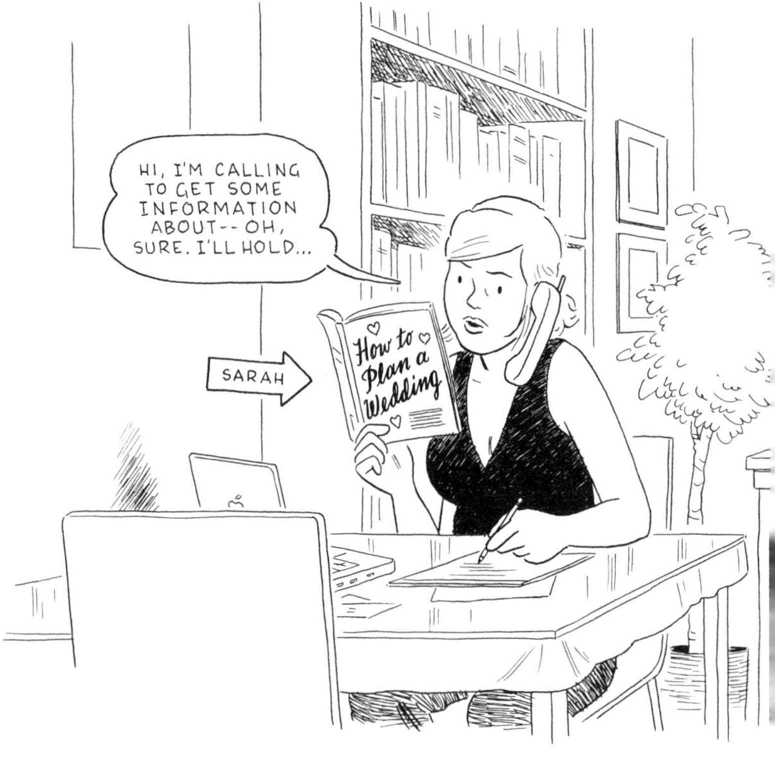
HI, I'M CALLING TO GET SOME INFORMATION ABOUT-- OH, SURE. I'LL HOLD...
SARAH
How to Plan a Wedding

Impending Marriage

a prenuptial memoir by ADRIAN TOMINE

DRAWN & QUARTERLY, publisher
MONTREAL

ALSO BY ADRIAN TOMINE

Sleepwalk and Other Stories

Summer Blonde

Shortcomings

32 Stories: The Complete Optic Nerve *Mini–Comics*

Scrapbook (Uncollected Work: 1990—2004)

Drawn & Quarterly
Post Office Box 48056
Montreal, Quebec
Canada H2V 4S8
www.drawnandquarterly.com

First edition: January 2011
Second printing: March 2011
Printed in Singapore

10 9 8 7 6 5 4 3 2

Library and Archives Canada Cataloguing in Publication
Tomine, Adrian, 1974-
Scenes from an impending marriage / Adrian Tomine.
ISBN 978-1-77046-034-8
I. Title.
PN6727.T65S24 2010   741.5'973   C2010-905762-7

Distributed in the USA by:
Farrar, Straus and Giroux
18 West 18th Street
New York, NY 10011
Orders: 888.330.8477

Distributed in Canada by:
Raincoast Books
2440 Viking Way
Richmond, BC V6V 1N2
Orders: 800.663.5714

www.adrian–tomine.com

For Nora

Guest List

THESE ARE THE ONLY PEOPLE YOU WANT TO INVITE?

YEP.

BUT WHAT ABOUT ▮▮▮▮ AND ▮▮▮▮?

THEY WOULDN'T WANT TO COME! THEY'D HAVE TO BRING THEIR KIDS ON A PLANE, GET TWO HOTEL ROOMS...

WELL, WE FLEW TO ▮▮▮▮ FOR **THEIR** WEDDING.

YEAH, AND I FELT OBLIGATED AND A LITTLE RESENTFUL!

NO, YOU DIDN'T!

BELIEVE ME: WE'RE DOING THEM A FAVOR BY **NOT** INVITING THEM!

OKAY, BUT WON'T THEY BE HURT IF THEY TALK TO ▮▮▮▮ AND FIND OUT THEY WEREN'T INVITED?

¡SIGH! NO GOOD DEED GOES UN- PUNISHED...

NOW WHY ISN'T ~~HEIDI~~ ON YOUR LIST?

ENH...SHE WOULDN'T WANT TO COME EITHER.

WHY ARE YOU PRE-EMPTIVELY MAKING THIS DECISION FOR EVERYONE? JUST INVITE HER!

WELL, SHE ALSO--

OH, NEVER MIND.

"SHE ALSO..." WHAT?

≶SIGH≷

I GAVE HER A COPY OF MY BOOK, AND SHE NEVER SAID ANYTHING ABOUT IT.

THAT IS OFFICIALLY THE MOST PATHETIC THING I'VE EVER HEARD.

SHE DIDN'T **LAVISH** YOU WITH PRAISE, SO SHE'S NOT INVITED TO YOUR WEDDING? HOW OLD ARE YOU?!

I WAS JUST KIDDING!

YEAH, RIGHT!

WELL, LET'S SEE **YOUR** LIST!

AH...LOOKS A BIT LONGER THAN MINE DOESN'T IT?

LET'S SEE... EX-BOYFRIEND WHO CHEATED ON YOU...

"PLUS GUEST," OBVIOUSLY.

...FRIEND YOU HAD A FALLING OUT WITH AND HAVEN'T SEEN IN THREE YEARS...

...CO-WORKERS YOU BARELY KNEW FROM A JOB YOU QUIT FIVE YEARS AGO...

ALL RIGHT!

FINE! I'LL TAKE ~~█████~~ AND ~~█████~~ OFF MY LIST, OKAY? BUT ~~████~~ IS STAYING ON!

AND I'LL ADD ~~██████~~ AND ~~█████~~ TO MY LIST, BUT NO WAY AM I INVITING ~~█████~~!

OKAY... HERE'S THE LIST OF PEOPLE OUR PARENTS WANT US TO INVITE.

IT'S LONGER THAN OUR TWO LISTS COMBINED! WHO ARE ALL THESE PEOPLE?!

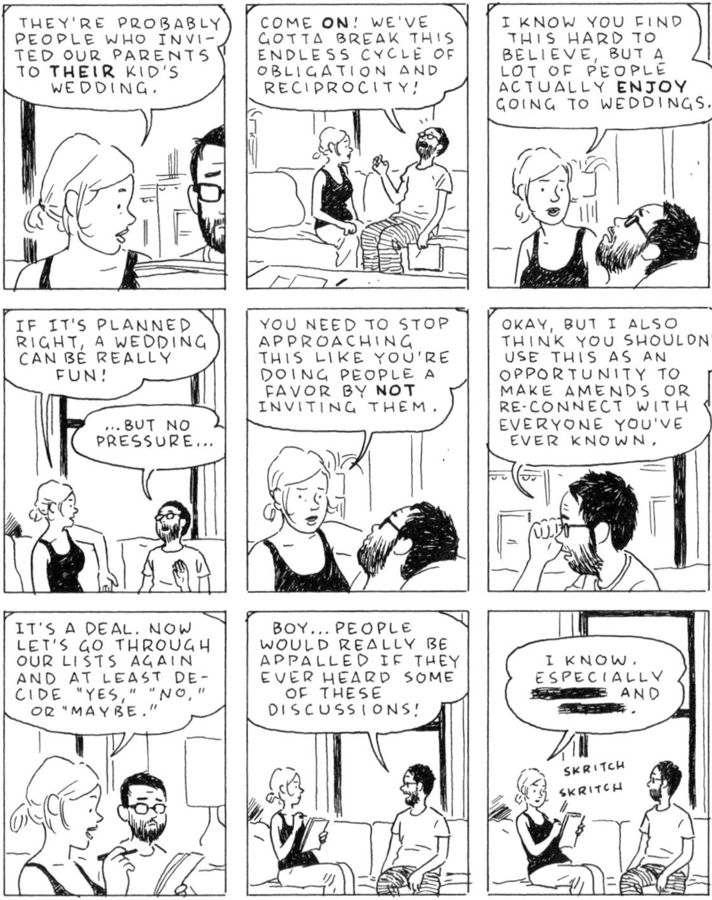
THEY'RE PROBABLY PEOPLE WHO INVITED OUR PARENTS TO **THEIR** KID'S WEDDING.
COME **ON**! WE'VE GOTTA BREAK THIS ENDLESS CYCLE OF OBLIGATION AND RECIPROCITY!
I KNOW YOU FIND THIS HARD TO BELIEVE, BUT A LOT OF PEOPLE ACTUALLY **ENJOY** GOING TO WEDDINGS.
IF IT'S PLANNED RIGHT, A WEDDING CAN BE REALLY FUN!
...BUT NO PRESSURE...
YOU NEED TO STOP APPROACHING THIS LIKE YOU'RE DOING PEOPLE A FAVOR BY **NOT** INVITING THEM.
OKAY, BUT I ALSO THINK YOU SHOULDN'T USE THIS AS AN OPPORTUNITY TO MAKE AMENDS OR RE-CONNECT WITH EVERYONE YOU'VE EVER KNOWN.
IT'S A DEAL. NOW LET'S GO THROUGH OUR LISTS AGAIN AND AT LEAST DECIDE "YES," "NO," OR "MAYBE."
BOY... PEOPLE WOULD REALLY BE APPALLED IF THEY EVER HEARD SOME OF THESE DISCUSSIONS!
I KNOW. ESPECIALLY [redacted] AND [redacted].
SKRITCH
SKRITCH

Reception Venue
FIRST OPTION:
...AND THIS IS WHERE YOU'D HAVE YOUR "RAW BAR." OF COURSE THE D.J. WOULD BE UP ON THE ROOF...
LET'S GO.
YEAH... IT'S A LITTLE OVER-THE-TOP, HUH?
WHAT DO YOU MEAN? IT'S MY FAVORITE COMBO: HIDEOUS **AND** EXPENSIVE!
SECOND OPTION:
NOW, BECAUSE THIS IS PART OF A STATE PARK, WE DON'T ALLOW HARD LIQUOR.
WE ALSO CAN'T ALLOW ANY CANDLES BECAUSE OF THE WILDFIRE HAZARD.
AND WHAT IF IT RAINS?
TCH!
"WHAT IF IT
"WHAT IF IT'S HOT?" "WHAT IF THERE'S MOSQUITOS?" "WHAT IF WE'RE FORCED TO ACTUALLY EXPERIENCE **NATURE** WHILE WE'RE OUTDOORS?"
SORRY. WE GET THESE QUESTIONS A LOT, AND I JUST...
FORGIVE ME.

Panel 1:
THIRD OPTION:

THE GREAT THING ABOUT A RAW SPACE LIKE THIS IS THAT IT'S ESSENTIALLY A BLANK CANVAS FOR YOUR CREATIVITY.

Panel 2:
HEY-- COME CHECK OUT THE VIEW OVER HERE.

Panel 3:
WHAT-- OH.

YEAH: FLOOR-TO-CEILING WINDOWS, LOOKING RIGHT OUT INTO "THE PROJECTS."

Panel 4:
OH, NO... THAT'S UNBELIEVABLE!

IT DOES KIND OF PUT THINGS IN PERSPEC-TIVE, HUH?

Panel 5:
CAN YOU IMAGINE LIVING IN THOSE BUILDINGS AND LOOKING INTO THESE WINDOWS EVERY NIGHT?

Panel 6:
CAN YOU IMAGINE DANCING AROUND IN HERE, SIPPING CHAMPAGNE, EAT-ING RIDICULOUS CATERED FOOD...?

Panel 7:
I THINK I'D RATHER THROW MYSELF OUT THE WINDOW!

Panel 8:
OKAY, HOLD ON. WOULD IT MAKE A DIFFERENCE IF I TOLD YOU THIS IS ONE-WAY GLASS?

TAP TAP TAP

Panel 9:
THE WEIRD GUY FROM THE PARK LEFT A MESSAGE SAYING THEY CAN PUT UP CANOPIES IF IT RAINS.

Exercise

"This nonsense stops the minute we're married!"

Invitation

SO, I DID SOME RESEARCH, AND THERE'S A STATIONERY STORE JUST DOWN THE STREET THAT MAKES NICE INVITATIONS.

WE'D MEET WITH ONE OF THE CONSULTANTS, LOOK AT SOME SAMPLES--

ARE YOU KIDDING? I CAN DESIGN AN INVITATION WITH MY EYES CLOSED!

I KNOW, BUT THEY HANDLE EVERYTHING; THE DESIGN, THE PRINTING...

COME ON.

THIS IS THE **ONE** PART OF THIS WHOLE PROCESS THAT I ACTUALLY KNOW SOMETHING ABOUT, SO LET ME DO IT.

THE NEXT DAY...

DONE!

CLIK

HMM... I THINK MAYBE THE BRIDE'S PARENTS SHOULD BE LISTED FIRST.

AND AREN'T YOU SUPPOSED TO SPELL THE DATE OUT, INSTEAD OF USING NUMBERS?

¿SIGH¿

OH, NEVER MIND. IT DOESN'T HAVE TO BE PERFECT.

ARGH! YOU **KNOW** THAT THE MINUTE YOU SAY THAT, I BECOME OBSESSED WITH MAKING IT PERFECT!

IT'S REALLY NOT A BIG--

YES IT IS! I'LL GOOGLE IT! I'LL FIGURE IT OUT!

FIVE HOURS LATER...

DONE!

THAT LOOKS GREAT!

THE NEXT DAY...

I GOT A PRICE QUOTE FROM THAT "OLD TIME-Y" PRINT SHOP.

WHOAH! YOU KNOW, I THINK THE PLACE DOWN THE STREET CAN DO IT FOR A LOT LESS.

YEAH, BUT CAN THEY DO AUTHENTIC HAND-SET TYPE AND LETTER-PRESS PRINTING?

UH...

I MEAN, IF YOU'RE GOING TO OUTPUT A TEXT-BASED FILE TO CHEAP OFFSET PRINTING, YOU MIGHT AS WELL GO TO KINKO'S!

TWO WEEKS LATER...

HELLO.

YOUR INVITATIONS ARE DONE,

GREAT! LET ME GIVE YOU OUR ADDRESS--

WE DON'T DELIVER. YOU PICK UP.

OH...WELL, WHAT SUBWAY STOP ARE YOU NEAR?

NONE. WALK OR TAKE A CAB.

WELL, THIS IS ANNOYING. BUT NO WAY AM I WASTING MONEY ON A CAB.

THEY'RE BEAUTIFUL!

THERE YOU GO: INVITATIONS, ENVELOPES, AND REPLY CARDS. SIGN HERE.

TAXI!

THE NEXT DAY...

I GUESS I'LL START ADDRESSING THESE ENVELOPES.

WHAT KIND OF PEN ARE YOU GONNA USE?

UH...I DON'T KNOW. BALL-POINT?

18

NO, NO, NO... IF YOU WANT THESE THINGS TO BE **PERFECT**, YOU NEED TO USE **THIS**!

BUT I NEVER SAID--

IT'S AN ANTIQUE CALLIGRAPHY PEN I BOUGHT ON EBAY!

BUT I DON'T KNOW HOW TO USE A CALLIGRAPHY PEN.

IT'S SIMPLE! IF YOU HOLD IT RIGHT, THE PEN DOES ALL THE HARD WORK FOR YOU.

SEE?

SKRITCH SKRITCH SKRITCH

WOW. THAT **IS** BEAUTIFUL. BUT I THINK I'M STILL BETTER OFF WITH A REGULAR BALL-POINT.

THREE DAYS LATER...

DONE!

ONE WEEK LATER, SOMEWHERE IN CALIFORNIA...

HEY... ADRIAN AND SARAH ARE GETTING MARRIED.

THAT'S NICE.

DID WE GET A NETFLIX?

19

An Even–Handed Acknowledgment of Both Families' Cultural Heritage

MY MOM ASKED IF WE WANT TO HAVE **TAIKO DRUMMERS** AT THE WEDDING.

CLICK

UH...OKAY. THAT MIGHT BE NICE.

YEAH, BUT REMEMBER? **YOUR** MOM WANTED BAGPIPE PLAYERS, AND WE NIXED THAT!

OH YEAH.

WELL, MAYBE WE SHOULD HAVE BOTH! THEY CAN "JAM" TOGETHER!

YEAH, THAT'S **EXACTLY** WHAT I WANT AT MY WEDDING: A BUNCH OF GUYS IN DIAPERS BANGING ON DRUMS AND A BUNCH OF GUYS IN SKIRTS BLOWING INTO BAGPIPES, ALL AT THE SAME TIME !!!

ALL RIGHT...TAKE IT EASY. YOU'RE CRACKING UNDER PRESSURE.

I JUST WISH THERE WAS SOME WAY TO MAKE EVERYONE HAPPY, INCLUDING US!

RELAX. EVERYONE **WILL** BE HAPPY. THIS STUFF IS ALL JUST ICING ON THE CAKE.

YOU'RE RIGHT. I DON'T KNOW WHY I GET SO NEUROTIC ABOUT THESE THINGS.

SO WHAT DO WE DO ABOUT THE, UH, MUSICAL ENTERTAINMENT SITUATION?

WELL, WE CAN'T HAVE ONE AND NOT THE OTHER.

IT'S TRUE. OKAY... IN THE NAME OF CULTURAL SENSITIVITY AND HARMONY...

...WE'LL HAVE NEITHER!

Seating Chart

*"I'm just saying it wouldn't <u>hurt</u> to create a
'buffer zone' between the quiet, sober, West Coast Asians
and the loud, drunken, East Coast Irish!"*

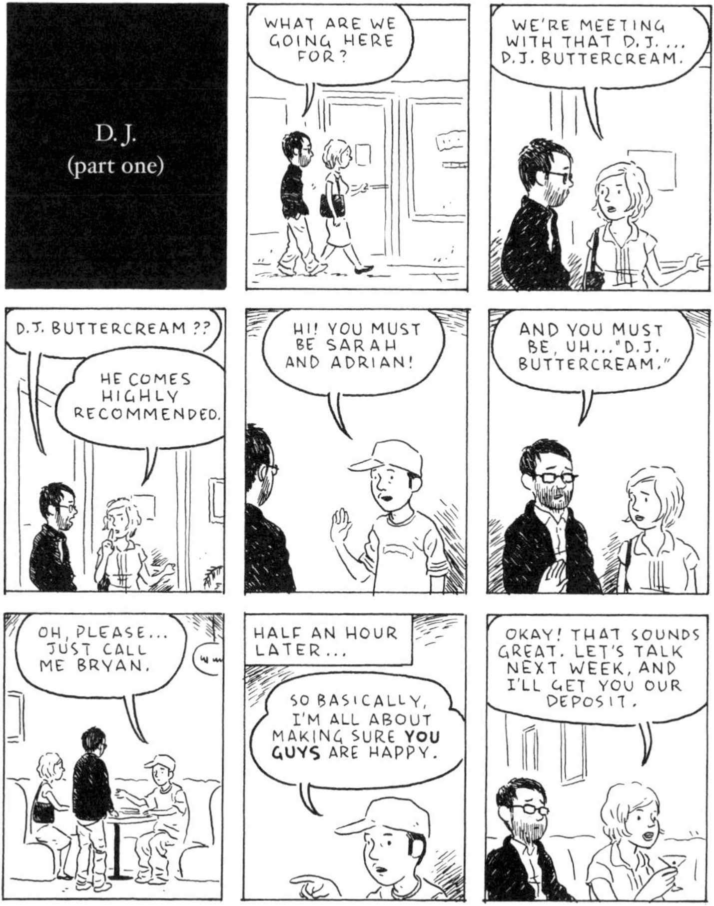
D. J.
(part one)
WHAT ARE WE GOING HERE FOR?
WE'RE MEETING WITH THAT D.J. ... D.J. BUTTERCREAM.
D.J. BUTTERCREAM??
HE COMES HIGHLY RECOMMENDED.
HI! YOU MUST BE SARAH AND ADRIAN!
AND YOU MUST BE, UH..."D.J. BUTTERCREAM."
OH, PLEASE... JUST CALL ME BRYAN.
HALF AN HOUR LATER...
SO BASICALLY, I'M ALL ABOUT MAKING SURE **YOU GUYS** ARE HAPPY.
OKAY! THAT SOUNDS GREAT. LET'S TALK NEXT WEEK, AND I'LL GET YOU OUR DEPOSIT.

GREAT! OH... AND TAKE A FEW OF MY MIX CDS. IT'LL JUST GIVE YOU A SENSE OF MY **FLOW**.

LATER...

BOY! THAT WAS KIND OF A HASTY DECISION YOU MADE...

WELL, I LIKED HIM. AND I DIDN'T SAY WE'D **DEFINITELY** HIRE HIM.

OH, I SEE.., SO WE'LL JUST SEND HIM A DEPOSIT FOR THE FUN OF IT!

THE NEXT DAY...

COME ON VOGUE

HEY! THESE MIX CDS THAT D.J. BUTTERCREAM MADE ARE **HORRIBLE**!

OH, DON'T BE SUCH A CRITICAL...

LOVE SHACK BABY!!

OH.

DAYS LATER...

UH, HI... BRYAN? IT'S SARAH...

HOW **ARE** YOU? SO, UH...IT TURNS OUT OUR BUDGET IS A BIT TIGHTER THAN EXPECTED, SO I'M AFRAID...

WHAT? OH, NO... WE'LL STILL HAVE MUSIC. WE'RE HIRING THIS **GREAT** BAND, AND...

YEAH, I GUESS TECHNICALLY A BAND **DOES** COST A LOT MORE THAN A D.J., BUT...

OOPS, I'VE GOT ANOTHER CALL! SORRY, BRYAN.

BYE.

CLICK

TWO MONTHS LATER...

HEY... WHO'S THAT GUY OVER THERE?

WHO?

OVER THERE. DON'T WE KNOW HIM FROM SOME- WHERE?

OH NO! IT'S D.J. BUTTERCREAM! AND HE'S STARING RIGHT AT US! DON'T LOOK!

HE'S NOT **STARING** AT US. WHY WOULD HE EVEN REMEMBER US?

DON'T LOOK!

SO WE DIDN'T HIRE HIM. BIG DEAL. I'M SURE HE DIDN'T TAKE IT PERSONALLY.

I JUST FEEL BAD. YOU KNOW I CAN'T BEAR THE THOUGHT OF ANYONE NOT LIKING ME!

YEAH... THAT'S WHERE WE DIFFER. JUST RELAX.

I CAN'T TAKE IT. LET'S GO.

WHAT?

ARE YOU SERIOUS?

THIS ISN'T EVEN OUR STOP!

Poor Us
(part one)

I HEARD ABOUT THIS CHARITY IN THE AREA.

MM-HM?

THEY NEED VOLUNTEERS TO COOK FOOD AND SERVE IT TO PEOPLE WITH H.I.V. AND AIDS.

HM.

I THOUGHT IT MIGHT BE A NICE THING FOR US TO DO.

WE'RE JUST SO BUSY WITH WEDDING STUFF RIGHT NOW, AND MONEY'S A LITTLE TIGHT...

OKAY. I GUESS YOU'RE RIGHT.

A MONTH LATER...

OH.

LOVE SHACK BABY!!

I GUESS WE'RE GONNA HAVE TO FIND A NEW D.J.! UGH, TURN IT OFF!

THE LOVE SHACK IS A LITTLE OLD PLACE

OH, THAT REMINDS ME...I'M GONNA HAVE TO FIND A NEW TAILOR.

DID YOU SEE WHAT THOSE *IDIOTS* DID TO MY SUIT? LOOK AT THIS!

AT LEAST YOU **HAVE** A SUIT! I'VE LOOKED AT A MILLION DRESSES AND THEY'RE ALL RIDICULOUS!

I TALKED TO THE CATERER, AND SHE SAID THAT CHICKEN **HAS** TO BE ONE OF THE ENTRÉE OPTIONS!

I TALKED TO THE PEOPLE AT THE CHURCH, AND THEY SAID THE SCAFFOLDING WOULD STILL BE UP!

UGH...WE STILL HAVE TO GO TO CRATE & BARREL AND REGISTER FOR STUFF!

OH, AND WE STILL HAVE TO FIGURE OUT WHAT TO GIVE AS FAVORS!

I'VE GOTTA HURRY UP AND BOOK OUR FLIGHTS TO HAWAII!

I DON'T KNOW WHO'S GONNA DO MY MAKE-UP!

WAAAAAAAAHH!!

LISTEN TO US. WHAT ARE WE DOING?

I SWORE I'D NEVER TURN INTO ONE OF "THOSE PEOPLE," AND NOW HERE WE ARE.

WE'RE GETTING SUCKED INTO A BLACK HOLE OF NUPTIAL NARCISSISM!

IF ANYONE COULD HEAR OUR WHINING, THEY'D HATE US!

I HATE US!

DO YOU THINK THEY STILL NEED HELP AT THAT AIDS DINNER?

Dance Lessons

"This nonsense stops the minute we're married!"

D. J.
(part two)

OKAY! WELL, I THINK WE'VE GOT EVERYTHING SQUARED AWAY.

I GOT THE PLAYLIST YOU EMAILED ME, SO THAT'S FINE.

GREAT.

AND I'M SORT OF A "MUSICOLOGIST," SO I HAD A FEW THOUGHTS.

WELL, I THINK WE'RE--

WE'D LOVE TO HEAR THEM!

WELL, I NOTICE YOU'VE PICKED A LOT OF OLDER STUFF...

CLICK CLICK

AND THAT MADE ME THINK OF THE BOB SEGER SONG "OLD TIME ROCK AND ROLL."

PFFFF

YEAH, MAYBE I SHOULD COME SLIDING INTO THE ROOM IN MY SOCKS AND UNDERPANTS!

"RISKY BUSINESS"!

SORRY. I THINK MAYBE WE SHOULD SKIP THAT ONE.

FINE. IT JUST SEEMED LIKE YOU GUYS LIKED OLD TIME ROCK AND ROLL, SO...

WE DO! WE JUST DON'T LIKE BOM-BASTIC SONGS **ABOUT** OLD TIME ROCK AND ROLL!

RIGHT...?

OKAY, WELL... ANOTHER SONG THAT I THOUGHT OF IS THE "ICE CREAM" SONG.

WHAT'S THAT?

UH...

OH! YOU DON'T KNOW IT? LOTS OF COUPLES USE IT FOR THEIR FIRST DANCE!

WELL, I THINK--

HERE... LISTEN!

CLICK CLICK CLICK

YOUR LO-O-O-OVE IS BETTER THAN ICE CREAM

OKAY, OKAY! I THINK WE GET THE IDEA!

I LO-O-OVE BETTER THAN CHOCOLATE

CLICK

UM...MAYBE WE SHOULD JUST STICK WITH OUR PLAYLIST.

WELL, WHAT I DO IS I GET A SENSE OF THE **VIBE**, THEN PICK THE RIGHT SONG FOR THE MOMENT.

WELL, CAN YOU JUST DO THAT WITHIN THE PARAMETERS OF OUR PLAYLIST?

SO BASICALLY YOU WANT AN iPOD SHUFFLE.

I'M SORRY IF WE'VE OFFENDED YOU. IT'S JUST...

HEY, I'LL PLAY WHATEVER YOU WANT. BUT I BET AN iPOD COULD DO IT JUST AS WELL.

CHEAPER, TOO!

Hundred Dollar Necktie

"...And you're <u>sure</u> I can't just wear the one
I bought for your grandma's funeral?"

Beauty Salon
Consultation

LET'S TRY OUT A FEW DIFFERENT HAIRSTYLES, AND THEN YOU CAN DECIDE WHAT'S BEST FOR THE BIG DAY.

OKAY, SOUNDS GREAT!

ONE HOUR LATER...

I LOVE IT!

THE SIDE-PART LOOKS GREAT, AND I REALLY LIKE THE, UH... FINGER-WAVES!

YOU SHOULD DEFINITELY GO WITH THIS STYLE. IT'S PERFECT!

THAT MUST BE YOUR FIANCE...?

UH, YEAH... THAT'S HIM.

WOW.

I'VE BEEN DOING THIS A LONG TIME, AND HE'S THE FIRST GUY WHO'S EVER COME TO THE CONSULTATION.

YOU'RE LUCKY YOU FOUND SUCH AN INVOLVED, SUPPORTIVE GUY!

HA!

PSSHT

WHILE HE **CAN** BE VERY SUPPORTIVE, THAT'S NOT REALLY WHY HE'S HERE.

OH?

THE TRUTH IS... HE'S JUST A CONTROL FREAK!

Registering

UGH...THIS ENTIRE STORE IS FILLED WITH HAPPY, YOUNG COUPLES "REGISTERING" FOR THEIR WEDDING!

IMAGINE HOW ANNOYING THIS WOULD BE IF YOU WERE SOME LONELY, SINGLE PERSON WHO JUST NEEDED A NEW BATH MAT!

WHAT A BIZARRE RITUAL! IT'S BASICALLY MAKING A LIST OF EXPENSIVE STUFF YOU EXPECT PEOPLE TO BUY FOR YOU!

AND WHAT'S WITH THESE BAR-CODE SCANNERS? IT LOOKS LIKE EVERYONE'S CASUALLY AIMING A GUN AT WICKER TISSUE BOX HOLDERS OR WHATEVER!

IT'S EMBLEMATIC OF OUR WHOLE CULTURE:"I WANT LOTS OF STUFF, AND I WANT TO SHOOT A GUN!"

AND YOU KNOW... NO ONE SEEMS EMBARRASSED OR—

ENOUGH!

JUST MAKE UP YOUR MIND: DO YOU LIKE THE "GRAND HOTEL" FLATWARE OR THE "CHARLEMAGNE"?

Florist

WE'VE GOTTA MAKE A DECISION ABOUT THE FLORIST.

OKAY. I THINK WE SHOULD GO WITH MIKI.

MIKI? SHE'S THE MOST EXPENSIVE! PLUS, SHE'S TOTALLY WEIRD!

WHO CARES? WE'RE NOT LOOK-ING TO BE **FRIENDS** WITH HER!

OKAY. I GET IT.

WHAT?

SHE'S JAPANESE.

YEAH... AND?

YOU ALWAYS JUST ASSUME THAT THE JAPAN-ESE PERSON IS THE BEST!

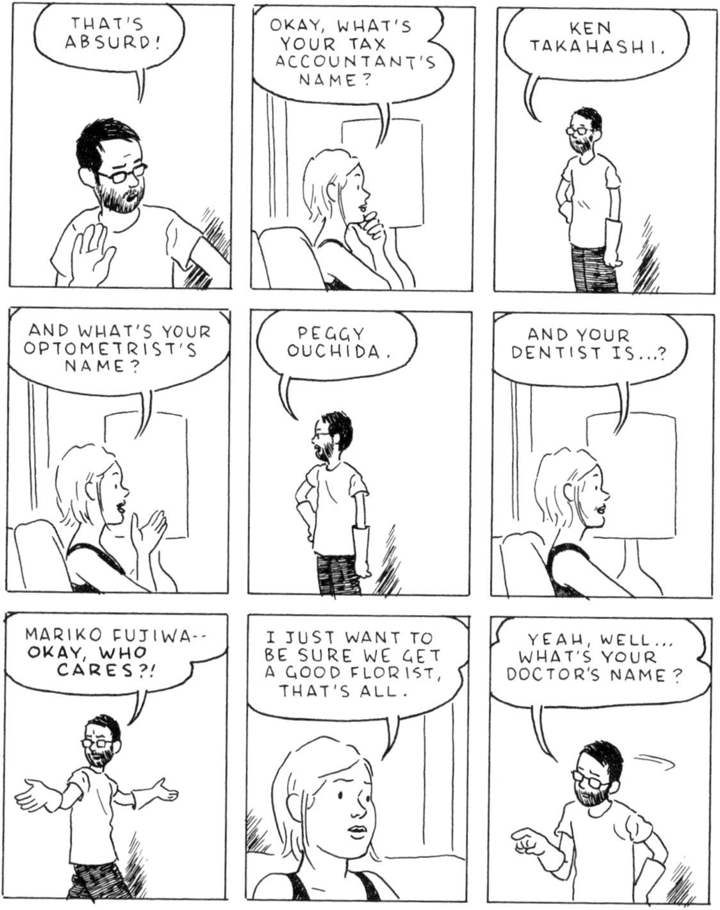
THAT'S ABSURD!
OKAY, WHAT'S YOUR TAX ACCOUNTANT'S NAME?
KEN TAKAHASHI.
AND WHAT'S YOUR OPTOMETRIST'S NAME?
PEGGY OUCHIDA.
AND YOUR DENTIST IS...?
MARIKO FUJIWA-- **OKAY, WHO CARES?!**
I JUST WANT TO BE SURE WE GET A GOOD FLORIST, THAT'S ALL.
YEAH, WELL... WHAT'S YOUR DOCTOR'S NAME?

YOU MEAN DR. O'FLAHERTY?

AH-**HAH**!

BUT THAT'S HER **MARRIED** NAME! SHE'S JEWISH.

ARE YOU SURE?

YES, BUT THAT'S NOT THE POINT! WE NEED TO PICK A FLORIST!

GO LOOK AT THE WEBSITES I SENT YOU AND DECIDE— **OBJECTIVELY**— WHO YOU LIKE BEST.

OKAY, OKAY...

MIKI!

Poor Us
(part two)

10:00 AM

WHERE DO YOU THINK WE SHOULD GO TO LOOK FOR MY WEDDING SOCKS?

WHAT? WE'RE NOT GOING SHOPPING TODAY.

WHY NOT?

WE'RE VOLUN-TEERING, REMEM-BER? THE DINNER FOR PEOPLE WITH AIDS AND H.I.V.?

THAT'S TODAY? BUT WHEN AM I GONNA LOOK FOR WEDDING SOCKS?

11:30 AM

I THOUGHT WE JUST WENT AND **SERVED** THE FOOD.

12:30 PM

THIS KITCHEN'S NOT BIG ENOUGH FOR ALL THIS COOKING!

2:30 PM

HOW FAR **IS** THIS PLACE?!

DO YOU THINK WE'LL HAVE TIME **AFTER** THIS TO LOOK FOR MY WEDDING SOCKS?

6:30 PM

¿WHEW¿

THAT WAS PRETTY INTENSE, HUH?

YEAH.

I DIDN'T THINK I'D BE SO SHAKEN UP.

SOME OF THOSE PEOPLE ARE SO SICK, AND THEY HAVE NO MONEY, NO INSURANCE, NO ONE TO TAKE CARE OF THEM...

I KIND OF THOUGHT THE PLACE WOULD BE OVERRUN WITH VOLUNTEERS...

BUT THEY WOULDN'T HAVE HAD ENOUGH FOOD TONIGHT WITHOUT THE STUFF WE BROUGHT.

WE SHOULD DO THIS EVERY MONTH.

YEAH.

ARE YOU OKAY?

WAAH!

Eyebrow Tweezing

"This nonsense stops the minute we're—OW! $#@&!!!"*

Favors

WHAT ARE YOU UP TO?

I'M LOOKING ONLINE FOR WEDDING FAVORS.

I GUESS I DON'T GET THE POINT OF THOSE THINGS.

IT'S JUST A LITTLE MEMENTO FOR PEOPLE TO TAKE HOME. IT'S NICE.

OKAY, OKAY... WHAT ARE SOME OF OUR OPTIONS?

WELL, THIS COMPANY MAKES CUSTOM CHOCOLATE BARS. WE CAN HAVE OUR NAMES PRINTED ON THEM.

BUT HOW IS THAT A "MEMENTO" IF IT'S JUST GONNA GET EATEN?

OKAY, SMARTY-PANTS. MAYBE YOU'D PREFER TO DRAW SOMETHING?

LIKE, MAYBE A SPECIAL CARD, OR...**OOH!** HOW ABOUT A LITTLE COMIC BOOK?

YOU MUST BE JOKING.

IT WOULD BE SO **CUTE!** YOU COULD DO A BUNCH OF SHORT STRIPS ABOUT US GETTING READY FOR THE WEDDING!

I DON'T HAVE TIME FOR SOMETHING LIKE THAT! LET'S JUST GET THE CHOCOLATE, AND—

OH! YOU COULD DO ONE ABOUT D.J. BUTTERCREAM! AND HOW ABOUT WHEN YOU CAME WITH ME TO THE SALON...

LOOK...EVERYONE LIKES CHOCOLATE! ESPECIALLY WHEN IT'S CUSTOMIZED! IT'S PERFECT!

IF YOU REALLY, REALLY, REALLY LOVED ME, YOU'D DO THIS.

:SIGH:

LET ME THINK ABOUT IT.

Epilogue

Old Time
Rock and Roll

WE DID IT!

I CAN'T BELIEVE WE'RE MARRIED!

I KNOW!

AND IT ALL WENT OFF WITHOUT A HITCH!

WELL, ALMOST.

OH.

THAT.

YEAH.

TWO HOURS EARLIER...

THIS NEXT SONG IS A SPECIAL REQUEST...

PIANO RIFF

WHAT THE...?

JUST TAKE THOSE OLD RECORDS OFF THE SHELF...

NOOOOO!

VERY FUNNY, BY THE WAY.

WHAT--?

I SWEAR: I DID NOT PUT THE D.J. UP TO THAT!

WELL, THEN SHE WAS STICKING IT TO ME.

WHAT?!

WHY ELSE WOULD SHE PLAY THE ONE SONG THAT I SPECIFICALLY ASKED HER **NOT** TO PLAY?

SHE SAID IT WAS A REQUEST!

YEAH...**RIGHT.** WHO WOULD'VE REQUESTED THAT SONG?

A LOT OF PEOPLE! THE DANCE FLOOR WAS PACKED! IT WAS FUN!

OKAY.

AT LEAST IT WASN'T THAT STUPID ICE CREAM SONG.

Honeymoon
Suite

WOW.

THIS IS BEAUTIFUL!

CHECK OUT THE VIEW!

AMAZING!

I LOVE YOU.

I LOVE YOU, TOO.

ALSO...

I'M **STARVING**.

ME TOO! I DIDN'T GET TO EAT ANYTHING ALL NIGHT!

I KNOW! FIRST WE HAD TO TAKE PHOTOS, THEN DO OUR DANCE, THEN GO AROUND AND SAY "HI" TO EVERYONE ...

EVERY TIME I'D RUSH BACK TO OUR TABLE, THEY WERE JUST CLEARING SOME AMAZING DISH AWAY!

IT WAS A TOTAL FORMER-FAT-KID NIGHTMARE!

OKAY, I'M CALLING ROOM SERVICE. WHAT DO YOU WANT?

BURGER AND FRIES?

YES!

BEEP BEEP BEEP

HI... I'D LIKE TO ORDER SOME ROOM SERVICE, PLEASE.

OH... REALLY?

HUH. OKAY...

WHAT.

NO ROOM SERVICE.

THEY HAVE A "CONTINENTAL BUFFET" IN THE MORNING, BUT THAT'S IT.

MAN... WHAT A DUMP!

After Hours

OKAY... FOOD.

IN A WEIRD PART OF TOWN.

AT 4:00 AM.

DAMN IT! EVERYTHING'S CLOSED.

COME ON... I'LL TAKE ANYTHING...

THANK YOU!

HI! CAN I GET TWO BURGERS, FRIES, ONION RINGS, AND TWO LARGE SODAS?

24

MY FIRST MEAL AS A MARRIED MAN!

CHEESE ON THE BURGERS?

JUST ON ONE. I'M, UH...

LACTOSE INTOLERANT...

EVENTUALLY...

HUFF

HUFF

DID SOMEONE ORDER A DISGUSTING ARRAY OF GREASY FOODS?

MY HERO!

SOME OF THIS STUFF LOOKS LIKE IT'S BEEN SITTING UNDER A HEAT LAMP SINCE LAST WEEK!

IT'S PERFECT.

CHOMP CHOMP DEVOUR CHEW

HOLY ▨▨▨. WE'RE MARRIED.

ADRIAN TOMINE was born in 1974 in Sacramento, California. He is the writer and artist of the comic book series *Optic Nerve*, as well as the books *Sleepwalk and Other Stories*, *Summer Blonde*, and *Shortcomings*. His comics and illustrations have appeared in *The New York Times* and *McSweeney's*, among others, and he is a frequent contributor to *The New Yorker*. He lives in Brooklyn with his wife and daughter.

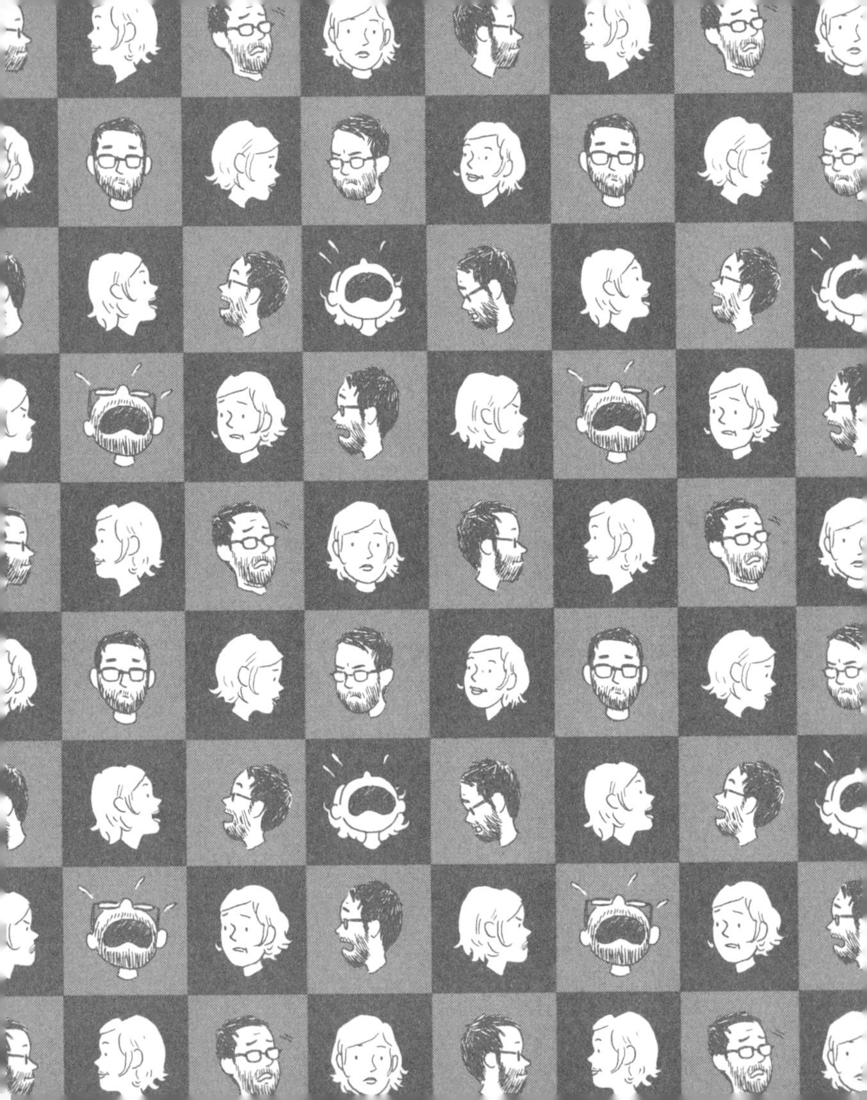